Poems of
Flowers

Poems of Flowers

Edited by Gail Harvey

GRAMERCY BOOKS
New York

Manufactured in Singapore
Designed by Melissa Ring

Library of Congress Cataloging-in-Publication Data
Poems of flowers / edited by Gail Harvey.
    p.   cm.
 ISBN 0-517-05323-3
    1. Flowers—Poetry.   2. English poetry.   3. American
poetry.
I. Harvey, Gail.
PN6110.F6P43   1991
821.008'036—dc20   90-39324
                                              CIP

8 7 6 5 4 3 2

Contents

Introduction

"*F*lowers," wrote Henry Ward Beecher, "have a mysterious and subtle influence upon the feelings." Indeed, flowers have the power to calm and to excite, to stimulate the imagination and to awaken memories. Flowers are messengers of love, of congratulations, of encouragement, and of condolence. They herald the arrival of spring, mark the passage of summer, and presage the onset of autumn. It is no wonder that poets have always extolled the beauty of flowers and mourned their fragility.

Poems of Flowers is a new collection of evocative poetry written by some of the world's greatest poets. Thomas Hood, for example, says that when the earth is sown with flowers " 'Tis like the birthday of the world." John Clare writes of the wonder of wild flowers "that dance to every wind," and Henry Wadsworth Longfellow describes flowers as "Stars, that in earth's firmament do shine." With charming whimsey Ben King takes us to The Flowers' Ball.

John Keats writes a sonnet of appreciation to a friend who sent him roses.

Emily Dickinson pays tribute to the purple clover and the mayflower, Robert Burns to the lilac, and Sir Walter Scott to the violet. William Blake writes movingly of the sunflower and Barry Cornwall of the snowdrop. William Wordsworth describes the wonder of a field of daffodils and Edwin Arnold welcomes the almond blossom, "April's gift to April bees, Birthday ornament of spring." Included, too, are wonderful poems by such great writers as Robert Frost, James Russell Lowell, William Cullen Bryant, Thomas Moore, and Percy Shelley.

This book is a paean to flowers, and, like a single perfect rose, a bouquet of fragrant lilac, or a bed of glowing tulips, these poems are sure to delight and bring happiness to all who read and reread them.

GAIL HARVEY

NEW YORK
1991

FLOWERS

I will not have the mad Clytie,
  Whose head is turned by the sun;
The tulip is a courtly quean,
  Whom, therefore, I will shun;
The cowslip is a country wench,
  The violet is a nun;—
But I will woo the dainty rose,
  The queen of every one.

The pea is but a wanton witch,
  In too much haste to wed,
And clasps her rings on every hand;
  The wolfsbane I should dread;
Nor will I dreary rosemary,
  That always mourns the dead;—
But I will woo the dainty rose,
  With her cheeks of tender red.

The lily is all in white, like a saint,
  And so is no mate for me;
And the daisy's cheek is tipped with a blush,
  She is of such low degree;
Jasmine is sweet, and has many loves,
  And the broom's betrothed to the bee;—
But I will plight with the dainty rose,
  For fairest of all is she.

Thomas Hood

ALMOND BLOSSOM

*B*lossom of the almond trees,
April's gift to April's bees,
Birthday ornament of spring,
Flora's fairest daughterling;—
Coming when no flow'rets dare
Trust the cruel outer air;
When the royal king-cup bold
Dares not don his coat of gold;
And the sturdy blackthorn spray
Keeps his silver for the May;—
Coming when no flow'rets would,
Save thy lowly sisterhood,
Early violets, blue and white,
Dying for their love of light.
Almond blossom, sent to teach us
That the spring days soon will reach us,
Lest, with longing over-tried,
We die as the violets died—
Blossom, clouding all the tree
With thy crimson broidery,
Long before a leaf of green
On the bravest bough is seen;
Ah! when winter winds are swinging
All thy red bells into ringing,
With a bee in every bell,
Almond bloom, we greet thee well.

EDWIN ARNOLD

FLOWER-GATHERING

I left you in the morning,
And in the morning glow
You walked a way beside me
To make me sad to go.
Do you know me in the gloaming,
Gaunt and dusty gray with roaming?
Are you dumb because you know me not,
Or dumb because you know?

All for me? And not a question
For the faded flowers gay
That could take me from beside you
For the ages of a day?
They are yours, and be the measure
Of their worth for you to treasure,
The measure of the little while
That I've been long away.

ROBERT FROST

THE BROOM FLOWER

O the broom, the yellow broom,
   The ancient poet sung it,
And dear it is on summer days
   To lie at rest among it.

I know the realms where people say
   The flowers have not their fellow;
I know where they shine out like suns,
   The crimson and the yellow.

I know where ladies live enchained
   In luxury's silken fetters,
And flowers as bright as glittering gems
   Are used for written letters.

But ne'er was flower so fair as this,
   In modern days or olden;
It groweth on its nodding stem
   Like to a garland golden.

And all about my mother's door
   Shine out its glittering bushes,
And down the glen, where clear as light
   The mountain water gushes.

Take all the rest; but give me this,
   And the bird that nestles in it;
I love it, for it loves the broom—
   The green and yellow linnet.

Well, call the rose the queen of flowers,
   And boast of that of Sharon,
Of lilies like to marble cups,
   And the golden rod of Aaron:

I care not how these flowers may be
   Beloved of man and woman;
The broom it is the flower for me,
   That groweth on the common.

O the broom, the yellow broom,
   The ancient poet sung it,
And dear it is on summer days
   To lie at rest among it.

MARY HOWITT

O LADY, LEAVE THY SILKEN THREAD

O Lady, leave thy silken thread
  And flowery tapestry,
There's living roses on the bush,
  And blossoms on the tree;
Stoop where thou wilt, thy careless hand
  Some random bud will meet;
Thou canst not tread, but thou wilt find
  The daisy at thy feet.

'Tis like the birthday of the world,
  When earth was born in bloom;
The light is made of many dyes,
  The air is all perfume;
There's crimson buds, and white and blue—
  The very rainbow showers
Have turned to blossoms where they fell,
  And sown the earth with flowers.

There's fairy tulips in the East,
  The garden of the sun;
The very streams reflect the hues,
  And blossom as they run:
While morn opes like a crimson rose,
  Still wet with pearly showers;
Then, Lady, leave the silken thread
  Thou twinest into flowers.

THOMAS HOOD

TO THE SMALL CELANDINE

*P*ansies, lilies, kingcups, daisies;
Let them live upon their praises;
Long as there's a sun that sets,
Primroses will have their glory;
Long as there are violets,
They will have a place in story:
There's a flower that shall be mine,
'Tis the little Celandine.

Eyes of some men travel far
For the finding of a star;
Up and down the heavens they go,
Men that keep a mighty rout!
I'm as great as they, I trow,
Since the day I found thee out,
Little flower!—I'll make a stir,
Like a sage astronomer.

Modest, yet withal an elf
Bold, and lavish of thyself;
Since we needs must first have met,
I have seen thee, high and low,
Thirty years or more, and yet
'T was a face I did not know;
Thou hast now, go where I may,
Fifty greetings in a day.

Ere a leaf is on a bush,
In the time before the thrush
Has a thought about her nest,
Thou wilt come with half a call,
Spreading out thy glossy breast
Like a careless prodigal;
Telling tales about the sun,
When we've little warmth, or none.

Poets, vain men in their mood!
Travel with the multitude:
Never heed them; I aver
That they all are wanton wooers;
But the thrifty cottager,
Who stirs little out of doors,
Joys to spy thee near at home;
Spring is coming, thou art come!

Comfort have thou of thy merit,
Kindly, unassuming spirit!
Careless of thy neighborhood,
Thou dost show thy pleasant face
On the moor, and in the wood,
In the lane;—there's not a place,
Howsoever mean it be,
But 't is good enough for thee.

Ill befall the yellow flowers,
Children of the flaring Hours!
Buttercups, that will be seen,
Whether we will see or no;
Others, too, of lofty mien;
They have done as worldlings do,
Taken praise that should be thine,
Little, humble Celandine.

Prophet of delight and mirth,
Ill-requited upon earth;
Herald of a mighty band,
Of a joyous train ensuing;
Serving at my heart's command,
Tasks that are no tasks renewing,
I will sing, as doth behoove,
Hymns in praise of what I love!

WILLIAM WORDSWORTH

PURPLE CLOVER

*T*here is a flower that bees prefer,
And butterflies desire;
To gain the purple democrat
The hummingbirds aspire.

And whatsoever insect pass,
A honey bears away
Proportioned to his several dearth
And her capacity.

Her face is rounder than the moon,
And ruddier than the gown
Of orchis in the pasture,
Or rhododendron worn.

She doth not wait for June;
Before the world is green
Her sturdy little countenance
Against the wind is seen,

Contending with the grass,
Near kinsman to herself,
For privilege of sod and sun,
Sweet litigants for life.

And when the hills are full,
And newer fashions blow,
Doth not retract a single spice
For pang of jealousy.

EMILY DICKINSON

TO THE CYCLAMEN

*T*hou Cyclamen of crumpled horn
  Toss not thy head aside;
Repose it where the Loves were born,
  In that warm dell abide.
Whatever flowers, on mountain, field,
  Or garden, may arise,
Thine only that pure odor yield
  Which never can suffice.
Emblem of her I've loved so long,
Go, carry her this little song.

WALTER SAVAGE LANDOR

THE TELL-TALE FLOWERS

*A*nd has the Spring's all glorious eye
    No lesson to the mind?
The birds that cleave the golden sky,
    Things to the earth resigned,
Wild flowers that dance to every wind,
Do they no memory leave behind?

Aye, flowers! The very name of flowers,
    That bloom in wood and glen,
Brings Spring to me in Winter's hours,
    And childhood's dreams again.
The primrose on the woodland lea
Was more than gold and lands to me.

The violets by the woodland side
    Are thick as they could thrive;
I've talked to them with childish pride
    As things that were alive:
I find them now in my distress,
They seem as sweet, yet valueless.

The cowslips on the meadow lea,
    How have I run for them!
I looked with wild and childish glee
    Upon each golden gem:
And when they bowed their heads so shy
I laughed, and thought they danced for joy.

And when a man, in early years,
    How sweet they used to come,
And give me tales of smiles and tears,
    And thoughts more dear than home:
Secrets which words would then reprove,
They told the names of early love.

The primrose turned a babbling flower
    Within its sweet recess:
I blushed to see its secret bower,
    And turned her name to bless.
The violets said the eyes were blue
I loved; and did they tell me true?

The cowslips, blooming everywhere,
    My heart's own thoughts could steal:
I nipt them that they should not hear:
    They smiled, and would reveal;
And o'er each meadow, right or wrong,
They sing the name I've worshipped long.

The brook that mirrored clear the sky,
    Full well I know the spot;
The mouse-ear looked with bright blue eye,
    And said "Forget-me-not."
And from the brook I turned away,
But heard it many an after day.

The king-cup on its slender stalk,
    Within the pasture dell,
Would picture there a pleasant walk
    With one I loved so well.
It said, "How sweet at eventide
'Twould be with true love at thy side."

And on the pasture's woody knoll
    I saw the wild bluebell,
On Sundays where I used to stroll
    With her I loved so well:
She culled the flowers the year before;
These bowed, and told the story o'er.

And every flower that had a name
    Would tell me who was fair;
But those without, as strangers, came
    And blossomed silent there:
I stood to hear, but all alone:
They bloomed and kept their thoughts unknown.

But seasons now have nought to say,
    The flowers no news to bring:
Alone I live from day to day,
    Flowers deck the bier of Spring;
And birds upon the bush or tree
All sing a different tale to me.

JOHN CLARE

DAFFODILS

I wandered, lonely as a cloud
That floats on high o'er vales and hills,
When all at once I saw a crowd—
A host of golden daffodils
Beside the lake, beneath the trees,
Flutt'ring and dancing in the breeze.

Continuous as the stars that shine
And twinkle on the milky way,
They stretched in never-ending line
Along the margin of a bay:
Ten thousand saw I, at a glance,
Tossing their heads in sprightly dance.

The waves beside them danced, but they
Outdid the sparkling waves in glee:
A poet could not but be gay,
In such a jocund company;
I gazed—and gazed—but little thought
What wealth the show to me had brought:

For oft, when on my couch I lie,
In vacant or in pensive mood,
They flash upon that inward eye
Which is the bliss of solitude,
And then my heart with pleasure fills,
And dances with the daffodils.

WILLIAM WORDSWORTH

WITH A PRESSED FLOWER

*T*his little flower from afar
Hath come from other lands to thine;
For, once, its white and drooping star
Could see its shadow in the Rhine.

Perchance some fair-haired German maid
Hath plucked one from the self-same stalk,
And numbered over, half afraid,
Its petals in her evening walk.

"He loves me, loves me not," she cries;
"He loves me more than earth or heaven!"
And then glad tears have filled her eyes
To find the number was uneven.

And thou must count its petals well,
Because it is a gift from me;
And the last one of all shall tell
Something I've often told to thee.

But here at home, where we were born,
Thou wilt find flowers just as true,
Down-bending every summer morn
With freshness of New England dew.

For Nature, ever kind to love,
Hath granted them the same sweet tongue,
Whether with German skies above,
Or here our granite rocks among.

JAMES RUSSELL LOWELL

I'D CHOOSE TO BE A DAISY

I'd choose to be a daisy,
　If I might be a flower,
Closing my petals softly
　At twilight's quiet hour;
And waking in the morning,
　When falls the early dew,
To welcome Heaven's bright sunshine,
　And Heaven's bright teardrops, too.

THE GARLAND I SEND THEE

*T*he garland I send thee was culled from those bowers
Where thou and I wandered in long vanished hours;
Not a leaf or a blossom its bloom here displays,
But bears some remembrance of those happy days.

The roses were gathered by that garden gate,
Where our meetings, though early, seemed always too late;
Where ling'ring full oft through a summer-night's moon,
Our partings, though late, appeared always too soon.

The rest were all culled from the banks of that glade,
Where, watching the sunset, so often we strayed,
And mourned, as the time went, that Love had no power
To bind in his chain even one happy hour.

THOMAS MOORE

TO THE DAISY

*W*ith little here to do or see
Of things that in the great world be,
Daisy! again I talk to thee,
　　For thou art worthy;—
Thou unassuming commonplace
Of Nature, with that homely face,
And yet with something of a grace,
　　Which love makes for thee!

Oft on the dappled turf at ease
I sit, and play with similes—
Loose types of things through all degrees,
　　Thoughts of thy raising;
And many a fond and idle name
I give to thee, for praise or blame,
As is the humor of the game,
　　While I am gazing.

A nun demure, of lowly port;
Or sprightly maiden of Love's court,
In thy simplicity the sport
　　Of all temptations;
A queen in crown of rubies drest;
A starveling in a scanty vest;
Are all, as seems to suit thee best,
　　Thy appellations.

A little cyclops with one eye
Staring to threaten and defy,
That thought comes next,—and instantly
   The freak is over;
The shape will vanish,—and behold
A silver shield with boss of gold
That spreads itself, some fairy bold
   In fight to cover!

I see thee glittering from afar,—
And then thou art a pretty star;
Not quite so fair as many are
   In heaven above thee!
Yet like a star, with glittering crest,
Self-poised in air thou seem'st to rest;—
May peace come never to his nest,
   Who shall reprove thee!

Bright flower! for by that name at last,
When all my reveries are past,
I call thee, and to that cleave fast,—
   Sweet, silent creature!
That breath'st with me in sun and air,
Do thou, as thou art wont, repair
My heart with gladness and a share
   Of thy meek nature!

WILLIAM WORDSWORTH

DANDELIONS

*S*ome young and saucy dandelions
　　Stood laughing in the sun;
They were brimming full of happiness,
　　And running o'er with fun.

At length they saw beside them
　　A dandelion old;
His form was bent and withered,
　　Gone were his locks of gold.

"Oh, oh!" they cried, "just see him;
　　"Old graybeard, how d'ye do?
We'd hide our heads in the grasses,
　　If we were as bald as you."

But lo! when dawned the morning,
　　Up rose each tiny head,
Decked not with golden tresses,
　　But long gray locks instead.

AUTHOR UNKNOWN

FRINGED GENTIAN

God made a little gentian;
It tried to be a rose
And failed, and all the summer laughed.
But just before the snows
There came a purple creature
That ravished all the hill;
And summer hid her forehead,
And mockery was still.
The frosts were her condition;
The Tyrian would not come
Until the North evoked it.
"Creator! shall I bloom?"

EMILY DICKINSON

THE WILD HONEYSUCKLE

*F*air flower, that dost so comely grow,
   Hid in this silent, dull retreat,
Untouched thy honeyed blossoms blow,
   Unseen thy little branches greet:
     No roving foot shall crush thee here,
     No busy hand provoke a tear.

By Nature's self in white arrayed,
   She bade thee shun the vulgar eye,
And planted here the guardian shade,
   And sent soft waters murmuring by
     Thus quietly thy summer goes—
     Thy days declining to repose.

Smit with those charms, that must decay
   I grieve to see your future doom;
They died—nor were those flowers more gay—
   The flowers that did in Eden bloom;
     Unpitying frosts, and Autumn's power
     Shall leave no vestige of this flower.

From morning suns and evening dews
   At first thy little being came:
If nothing once, you nothing lose,
   For when you die you are the same;
     The space between is but an hour,
     The frail duration of a flower.

PHILIP FRENEAU

THE IRIS

*T*hou art the Iris, fair among the fairest,
    Who, armed with golden rod
And winged with the celestial azure, bearest
    The message of some God.

Thou art the Muse, who far from crowded cities
    Hauntest the sylvan streams,
Playing on pipes of reed the artless ditties
    That come to us as dreams.

O flower-de-luce, bloom on, and let the river
    Linger to kiss thy feet!
O flower of song, bloom on, and make for ever
    The world more fair and sweet.

HENRY WADSWORTH LONGFELLOW

THE FLOWERS' BALL

*T*here is an olden story,
   'Tis a legend, so I'm told,
How the flowerets gave a banquet,
   In the ivied days of old;
How the posies gave a party once
   That wound up with a ball,
How they held it in a valley,
   Down in "Flowery Kingdom Hall."

The flowers of every clime were there,
   Of high and low degree,
All with their petals polished,
   In sweet aromatic glee.
They met down in this woodland
   In the soft and ambient air,
Each in its lolling loveliness,
   Exhaled a perfume rare.

An orchestra of Blue Bells
   Sat upon a mossy knoll
And pealed forth gentle music
   That quite captured every soul.
The Holly hocked a pistil
   Just to buy a suit of clothes,
And danced with all the flowerets
   But the modest, blushing Rose.

The Morning Glory shining
  Seemed reflecting all the glow
Of dawn, and took a partner;
  It was young Miss Mistletoe.
Miss Maggie Nolia from the South
  Danced with Forget-me-not;
Sweet William took Miss Pink in tow
  And danced a slow gavotte.

Thus everything went swimmingly
  'Mongst perfumed belles and beaux,
And every floweret reveled save
  The modest, blushing Rose.
Miss Fuchsia sat around and told
  For floral emulation,
That she had actually refused
  To dance with A. Carnation.

The Coxcomb, quite a dandy there,
  Began to pine and mope,
Until he had been introduced
  To young Miss Heliotrope.
Sir Cactus took Miss Lily,
  And he swung her so about
She asked Sweet Pea to Cauliflower
  And put the Cactus out.

Miss Pansy took her Poppy
   And she waltzed him down the line
Till they ran against old Sunflower
   With Miss Honeysuckle Vine.
The others at the party that
   Went whirling through the mazy
Were the Misses Rhodo Dendron,
   Daffodil and little Daisy.

Miss Petunia, Miss Verbena, Violet,
   And sweet Miss Dahlia
Came fashionably late, arrayed
   In very rich regalia.
Miss Begonia, sweet Miss Buttercup,
   Miss Lilac and Miss Clover;
Young Dandelion came in late
   When all the feast was over.

The only flower that sent regrets
   And really couldn't come,
Who lived in the four hundred, was
   The vain Chrysanthemum.
One floweret at the table
   Grew quite ill, we must regret,
And every posy wondered, too,
   Just what Miss Mignonette.

Young Tulip chose Miss Orchid
   From the first, and did not part
With her until Miss Mary Gold
   Fell with a Bleeding Heart.
But ah! Miss Rose sat pensively
   Till every young bud passed her;
When just to fill the last quadrille,
   The little China Aster.

BEN KING

THE LILAC

O were my Love you lilac fair,
    Wi' purple blossoms to the spring,
And I a bird to shelter there,
    When wearied on my little wing;
How I wad mourn when it was torn
    By autumn wild and winter rude!
But I wad sing on wanton wing
    When youthfu' May its bloom renew'd.

Robert Burns

HOW MARIGOLDS CAME YELLOW

*J*ealous girls these sometimes were,
While they lived, or lasted here:
Turned to flowers, still they be
Yellow, marked for jealousy.

ROBERT HERRICK

MAYFLOWER

*P*ink, small, and punctual,
Aromatic, low,
Covert in April,
Candid in May,

Dear to the moss,
Known by the knoll,
Next to the robin
In every human soul.

Bold little beauty,
Bedecked with thee,
Nature forswears
Antiquity.

EMILY DICKINSON

ONE PANSY

One Pansy, one, she bore beneath her breast,
    A broad white ribbon held that Pansy tight.
She waved about nor looked upon the rest,
    Costly and rare; on this she bent her sight.
I watched her raise it gently when it drooped;
    I knew she wished to show it me; I knew
She would I saw it rise, to lie unlooped
    Nearer its home, that tender heart! that true!

WALTER SAVAGE LANDOR

THE POPPY

*S*ummer set lip to earth's bosom bare,
  And left the flushed print in a poppy there:
Like a yawn of fire from the grass it came,
  And the fanning wind puffed it to flapping flame.

With burnt mouth red like a lion's it drank
  The blood of the sun as he slaughtered sank,
And dipped its cup in the purpurate shine
  When the eastern conduits ran with wine;

Till it grew lethargied with fierce bliss,
  And hot as a swinkèd gypsy is,
And drowsed in sleepy savageries,
  With mouth wide a-pout for a sultry kiss.

A child and man paced side by side,
  Treading the skirts of eventide;
But between the clasp of his hand and hers
  Lay, felt not, twenty withered years.

FRANCIS THOMPSON

THE PRIMROSE

*A*sk me why I send you here
This sweet infanta of the year?
   Ask me why I send to you
This Primrose, thus bepearled with dew?
   I will whisper to your ears,
The sweets of love are mixed with tears.

   Ask me why this flower does show
So yellow-green, and sickly too?
   Ask me why the stalk is weak
And bending, (yet it doth not break?)
   I will answer, These discover
What fainting hopes are in a lover.

ROBERT HERRICK

RED AND WHITE ROSES

*R*ead in these roses the sad story
Of my hard fate, and your own glory.
  In the white you may discover
  The paleness of a fainting lover;
In the red the flames still feeding
On my heart, with fresh wounds bleeding.
  The white will tell you how I languish,
  And the red express my anguish;
The white my innocence displaying,
The red my martyrdom betraying.
  The frowns that on your brow resided,
  Have those roses thus divided.
Oh! let your smiles but clear the weather,
And then they both shall grow together.

THOMAS CAREW

FLOWERS

*E*re yet our course was graced with social trees
It lacked not old remains of hawthorn bowers,
Where small birds warbled to their paramours;
And, earlier still, was heard the hum of bees;
I saw them ply their harmless robberies,
And caught the fragrance which the sundry flowers,
Fed by the stream with soft perpetual showers,
Plenteously yielded to the vagrant breeze.
There bloomed the strawberry of the wilderness;
The trembling eyebright showed her sapphire blue,
The thyme her purple, like the blush of Even;
And if the breath of some to no caress
Invited, forth they peeped so fair to view,
All kinds alike seemed favorites of Heaven.

WILLIAM WORDSWORTH

ASKING FOR ROSES

A house that lacks, seemingly, mistress and master,
  With doors that none but the wind ever closes,
Its floor all littered with glass and with plaster;
  It stands in a garden of old-fashioned roses.

I pass by that way in the gloaming with Mary;
  "I wonder," I say, "who the owner of those is."
"Oh, no one you know," she answers me airy,
  "But one we must ask if we want any roses."

So we must join hands in the dew coming coldly
  There in the hush of the wood that reposes,
And turn and go up to the open door boldly,
  And knock to the echoes as beggars for roses.

"Pray, are you within there, Mistress Who-were-you?"
  'Tis Mary that speaks and our errand discloses.
"Pray, are you within there? Bestir you, bestir you!
  'Tis summer again; there's two come for roses.

"A word with you, that of the singer recalling—
  Old Herrick: a saying that every maid knows is
A flower unplucked is but left to the falling,
  And nothing is gained by not gathering roses."

We do not loosen our hands' intertwining
  (Not caring so very much what she supposes),
There when she comes on us mistily shining
  And grants us by silence the boon of her roses.

Robert Frost

SONNET

*M*y lady's presence makes the Roses red,
Because to see her lips they blush for shame;
The Lily's leaves, for envy, pale became,
For her white hands in them this envy bred.
The Marigold the leaves abroad doth spread,
Because the Sun's and her power is the same;
The Violet of purple color came,
Dyed in the blood she made my heart to shed.
In brief, all flowers from her their virtue take;
From her sweet breath their sweet smells do proceed;
The living heat which her eyebeams do make
Warmeth the ground, and quickeneth the seed.
The rain, wherewith she watereth the flowers,
Falls from mine eyes, which she dissolves in showers.

HENRY CONSTABLE

TO A FRIEND WHO SENT ME SOME ROSES

*A*s late I rambled in the happy fields,
   What time the skylark shakes the tremulous dew
   From his lush clover covert;—when anew
Adventurous knights take up their dinted shields:
I saw the sweetest flower wild nature yields,
   A fresh-blown musk rose; 'twas the first that threw
   Its sweets upon the summer: graceful it grew
As is the wand that queen Titania wields.
And, as I feasted on its fragrancy:
   I thought the garden rose it far excell'd:
But when, O Wells! thy roses came to me
   My sense with their deliciousness was spell'd:
Soft voices had they, that with tender plea
   Whisper'd of peace, and truth, and friendliness
         unquell'd.

JOHN KEATS

TO THE SNOWDROP

*P*retty firstling of the year!
  Herald of the host of flowers!
Hast thou left thy cavern drear,
  In the hope of summer hours?
  Back unto thy earthen bowers!
Back to thy warm world below,
  Till the strength of suns and showers
Quell the now relentless snow!

Art *still* here?—Alive? and blithe?
  Though the stormy night hath fled,
And the frost hath passed his scythe
  O'er thy small, unsheltered head?
  Ah!—some lie amidst the dead,
(Many a giant, stubborn tree,—
  Many a plant, its spirit shed,)
That were better nursed than thee!

What hath saved thee? Thou wast not
   'Gainst the arrowy winter furred,—
Armed in scale,—but all forgot
   When the frozen winds were stirred.
   Nature, who doth clothe the bird,
Should have hid thee in the earth,
   Till the cuckoo's song was heard,
And the Spring let loose her mirth.

   Nature,—deep and mystic word!
   Mighty mother, still unknown!
Thou didst sure the snowdrop gird
   With an armor all thine own!
   Thou, who sent'st it forth alone
To the cold and sullen season,
   (Like a thought at random thrown,)
Sent it thus for some grave reason!

If 't were but to pierce the mind
   With a single, gentle thought,
Who shall deem thee harsh or blind
   Who that thou hast vainly wrought?
   Hoard the gentle virtue caught
From the snowdrop,—reader wise!
   Good is good, wherever taught,
On the ground or in the skies!

Barry Cornwall

AH! SUNFLOWER

*A*h Sunflower! weary of time,
Who countest the steps of the Sun,
Seeking after that sweet golden clime
Where the traveller's journey is done:

Where the Youth pined away with desire,
And the pale Virgin shrouded in snow
Arise from their graves and aspire
Where my Sunflower wishes to go.

WILLIAM BLAKE

TO A BED OF TULIPS

*B*right tulips, we do know
You had your coming hither;
And fading-time does show,
That ye must quickly wither.

Your sister-hoods may stay,
And smile here for your hour;
But die ye must away:
Even as the meanest flower.

Come Virgins then, and see
Your frailties; and bemoan ye;
For lost like these, 'twill be,
As Time had never known ye.

ROBERT HERRICK

ROSE POGONIAS

A saturated meadow,
  Sun-shaped and jewel-small,
A circle scarcely wider
  Than the trees around were tall;
Where winds were quite excluded,
  And the air was stifling sweet
With the breath of many flowers—
  A temple of the heat.

There we bowed us in the burning,
  As the sun's right worship is,
To pick where none could miss them
  A thousand orchises;
For though the grass was scattered,
  Yet every second spear
Seemed tipped with wings of color,
  That tinged the atmosphere.

We raised a simple prayer
  Before we left the spot,
That in the general mowing
  That place might be forgot;
Or if not all so favored,
  Obtain such grace of hours,
That none should mow the grass there
  While so confused with flowers.

ROBERT FROST

THE VIOLET

*T*he violet in her green-wood bower,
   Where birchen boughs with hazels mingle,
May boast itself the fairest flower
   In glen, or copse, or forest dingle.

Though fair her gems of azure hue,
   Beneath the dewdrop's weight reclining;
I've seen an eye of lovelier blue,
   More sweet through wat'ry luster shining.

The summer sun that dew shall dry,
   Ere yet the day be past its morrow;
Nor longer in my false love's eye
   Remained the tear of parting sorrow.

Sir Walter Scott

FLOWERS

Spake full well, in language quaint and olden,
  One who dwelleth by the castled Rhine,
When he called the flowers, so blue and golden,
  Stars, that in earth's firmament do shine.

Stars they are, wherein we read our history,
  As astrologers and seers of old;
Yet not wrapped about with awful mystery,
  Like the burning stars which they beheld.

Wondrous truths, and manifold as wondrous,
  God hath written in those stars above;
But not less in the bright flowerets under us
  Stands the revelation of his love.

Bright and glorious is that revelation,
  Writ all over this great world of ours—
Making evident our own creation,
  In these stars of earth, these golden flowers.

And the poet, faithful and far-seeing,
  Sees, alike in stars and flowers, a part
Of the self-same, universal being
  Which is throbbing in his brain and heart.

Gorgeous flowerets in the sunlight shining,
  Blossoms flaunting in the eye of day,
Tremulous leaves, with soft and silver lining,
  Buds that open only to decay;

Brilliant hopes, all woven in gorgeous tissues,
  Flaunting gayly in the golden light;
Large desires, with most uncertain issues,
  Tender wishes, blossoming at night!

These in flowers and men are more than seeming;
    Workings are they of the self-same powers
Which the poet, in no idle dreaming,
    Seeth in himself and in the flowers.

Everywhere about us are they glowing—
    Some, like stars, to tell us Spring is born;
Others, their blue eyes with tears o'erflowing,
    Stand, like Ruth, amid the golden corn.

Not alone in Spring's armorial bearing,
    And in Summer's green-emblazoned field,
But in arms of brave old Autumn's wearing,
    In the center of his brazen shield;

Not alone in meadows and green alleys,
    On the mountaintop, and by the brink
Of sequestered pools in woodland valleys,
    Where the slaves of Nature stoop to drink;

Not alone in her vast dome of glory,
    Not on graves of bird and beast alone,
But in old cathedrals, high and hoary,
    On the tombs of heroes, carved in stone;

In the cottage of the rudest peasant;
    In ancestral homes, whose crumbling towers,
Speaking of the Past unto the Present,
    Tell us of the ancient Games of Flowers.

In all places, then, and in all seasons,
    Flowers expand their light and soul-like wings,
Teaching us, by most persuasive reasons,
    How akin they are to human things.

And with childlike, credulous affection,
    We behold their tender buds expand—
Emblems of our own great resurrection,
    Emblems of the bright and better land.

HENRY WADSWORTH LONGFELLOW

THE YELLOW VIOLET

*W*hen beechen buds begin to swell,
  And woods the bluebird's warble know,
The yellow violet's modest bell
  Peeps from the last year's leaves below.

Ere russet fields their green resume,
  Sweet flower, I love, in forest bare,
To meet thee, when thy faint perfume
  Alone is in the virgin air.

Of all her train, the hands of Spring
  First plant thee in the watery mold,
And I have seen thee blossoming
  Beside the snowbank's edges cold.

Thy parent sun, who bade thee view
  Pale skies, and chilling moisture sip,
Has bathed thee in his own bright hue,
  And streaked with jet thy glowing lip.

Yet slight thy form, and low thy seat,
  And earthward bent thy gentle eye,
Unapt the passing view to meet
  When loftier flowers are flaunting nigh.

Oft, in the sunless April day,
  Thy early smile has stayed my walk;
But midst the gorgeous blooms of May,
  I passed thee on thy humble stalk.

So they, who climb to wealth, forget
  The friends in darker fortunes tried.
I copied them—but I regret
  That I should ape the ways of pride.

And when again the genial hour
  Awakes the painted tribes of light,
I'll not o'erlook the modest flower
  That made the woods of April bright.

WILLIAM CULLEN BRYANT

THE WILD FLOWER'S SONG

*A*s I wandered the forest,
The green leaves among,
I heard a wild flower
Singing a song.

"I slept in the Earth
In the silent night,
I murmured my fears
And I felt delight.

"In the morning I went,
As rosy as morn,
To seek for new Joy;
But I met with scorn."

WILLIAM BLAKE

SONNET

Written in a country retirement

*A*round my porch and lonely casement spread,
The myrtle never sere, and gadding vine,
With fragrant sweet-briar love to intertwine;
And in my garden's box-encircled bed
The pansy pied, and musk rose white and red;
The pink, the lily chaste, and sweet woodbine,
Fling odors round; thick-woven eglantine
Decks my trim fence; in which, by silence led,
The wren hath wisely built her mossy cell,
Shelter'd from storms, in courtly land so rife,
And nestles o'er her young, and warbles well.
'Tis here with innocence in peaceful glen
I pass my blameless moments far from men,
Nor wishing death too soon, nor asking life.

JOHN CODRINGTON BAMPFYLDE

AT THE CLOSE OF SPRING

The garlands fade that Spring so lately wove,
  Each simple flower which she had nursed in dew,
Anemones that spangled every grove,
  The primrose wan, and harebell mildly blue.
No more shall violets linger in the dell,
  Or purple orchis variegate the plain,
Till Spring again shall call forth every bell,
  And dress with humid hands her wreaths again.
Ah! poor humanity! so frail, so fair,
  Are the fond visions of thy early day,
Till tyrant passion and corrosive care
  Bid all thy fairy colors fade away!
Another May new buds and flowers shall bring;
Ah! why has happiness no second Spring?

CHARLOTTE SMITH

ON A FADED VIOLET

I

*T*he odor from the flower is gone
  Which like thy kisses breathed on me;
The color from the flower is flown
  Which glowed of thee and only thee!

II

A shrivelled, lifeless, vacant form,
  It lies on my abandoned breast,
And mocks the heart which yet is warm,
  With cold and silent rest.

III

I weep,—my tears revive it not!
  I sigh,—it breathes no more on me;
Its mute and uncomplaining lot
  Is such as mine should be.

PERCY SHELLEY

A CONTEMPLATION UPON FLOWERS

*B*rave flowers—that I could gallant it like you,
    And be as little vain!
You come abroad, and make a harmless show,
    And to your beds of earth again.
You are not proud: you know your birth:
For your embroidered garments are from earth.

You do obey your months and times, but I
    Would have it ever Spring:
My fate would know no Winter, never die,
    Nor think of such a thing.
O that I could my bed of earth but view
And smile, and look as cheerfully as you!

O teach me to see Death and not to fear,
    But rather to take truce!
How often have I seen you at a bier,
    And there look fresh and spruce!
You fragrant flowers! then teach me, that my breath
Like yours may sweeten and perfume my death.

HENRY KING, BISHOP OF CHICHESTER

FLOWER IN THE CRANNIED WALL

*F*lower in the crannied wall,
I pluck you out of the crannies,
I hold you here, root and all, in my hand,
Little flower—but *if* I could understand
What you are, root and all, and all in all,
I should know what God and man is.

ALFRED, LORD TENNYSON